Talking to Angels

Talking to Angels

ESTHER WATSON

Harcourt Brace & Company

SAN DIEGO   NEW YORK   LONDON

Requests for permission to make copies

of any part of the work should be mailed to:

Permissions Department, Harcourt Brace & Company,

6277 Sea Harbor Drive, Orlando, Florida 32887-6777.

PRINTED IN SINGAPORE

Library of Congress Cataloging-in-Publication Data

Watson, Esther.

Talking to angels/Esther Watson.

p.   cm.

ISBN 0-15-201077-7

1. Autistic children—Juvenile literature.

[1. Autism.]   I. Title

RJ506.A9W38   1996

618.92'8982—dc20   95-30913

First edition

A B C D E

FOR CHRISTA

CHRISTA likes to do what I do.

She even likes to say what I say.

When she puts her hands on
my cheeks and looks in my eyes,
I repeat every word she says.
That makes her laugh.

She hears what I say, only she answers back in her head. She doesn't speak to me out loud.

Christa loves the way water looks.

She also likes the way
kittens feel on her cheek.

Sometimes if I sit very still, I can
hear Christa softly talking to angels.
I don't know what she is saying,
but it sounds important.

Christa covers her ears when she hears bad noises. That means "Stop that noise."

She cries when she sees others crying.

And some people don't
understand what she stares at.

Sometimes she hears something
so beautiful she stops what she
is doing and just listens.

My sister Christa is autistic.

And she is my best friend, too.

The illustrations in this book were done in

mixed media on drawing paper.

The display type was hand-lettered by Esther Watson.

The text type was set in Spectrum.

Color separations by Bright Arts, Ltd., Singapore

Printed and bound by Tien Wah Press, Singapore

This book was printed with soya-based inks on

Leykam recycled paper, which contains more than

20 percent postconsumer waste and has a total

recycled content of at least 50 percent.

Production supervision by Warren Wallerstein

and Ginger Boyer

Designed by Michael Farmer